damien rice 4

I can't stay here
I can, but I shouldn't
it's not that I shouldn't, but I don't think I should
I want to, but I don't want to, but I shouldn't want to
Though, it's not that I shouldn't want to
but I don't, yet I do, but I don't really
so I shouldn't
so I won't
so don't be hurt
'cause you shouldn't

Bederick

written by damien rice

paintings & drawings by fred + daisy

©2007 by Faber Music Ltd
First published by Faber Music Ltd in 2007
3 Queen Square, London WC1N 3AU

Arranged by Alex Davis
Engraved by Camden Music
Edited by Lucy Holliday

Printed in England by Caligraving Ltd

ISBN10: 0-571-52842-2
EAN13: 978-0-571-52842-4

To buy Faber Music publications or to find out about
the full range of titles available, please contact your
local music retailer or Faber Music sales enquiries:

Faber Music Ltd, Burnt Mill, Elizabeth Way,
Harlow, CM20 2HX England
Tel: +44(0)1279 82 89 82 Fax: +44(0)1279 82 89 83
sales.fabermusic.com fabermusic.com

damien rice 9

9 CRIMES

Words and Music by Damien Rice

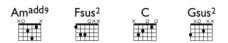

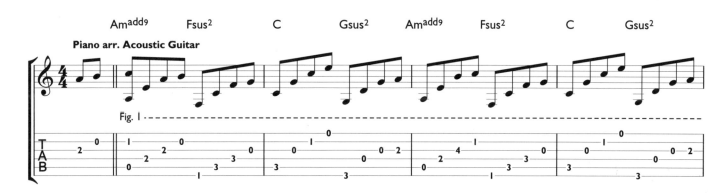

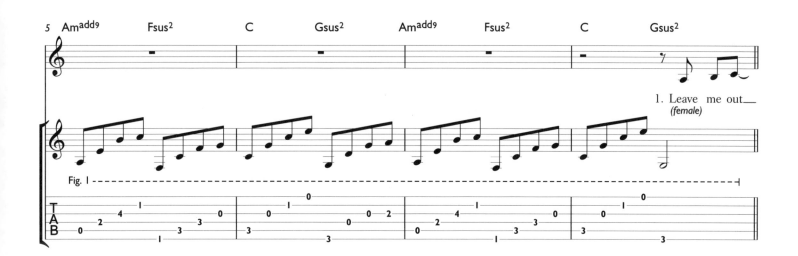

1. Leave me out _____
(female)

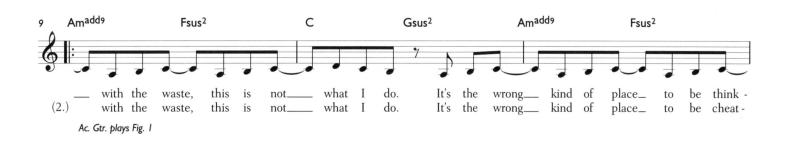

(2.) with the waste, this is not ___ what I do. It's the wrong ___ kind of place ___ to be think-
_____ with the waste, this is not ___ what I do. It's the wrong ___ kind of place ___ to be cheat-

Ac. Gtr. plays Fig. I

- ing of you. It's the wrong _____ time ___ for some-bo-dy new. It's a small ___
- ing on you. It's the wrong _____ time, ___ she's pul-ling me through. It's a small ___

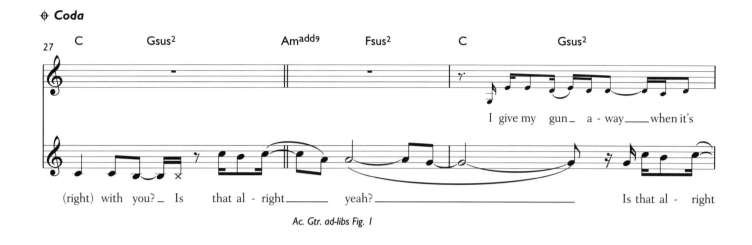

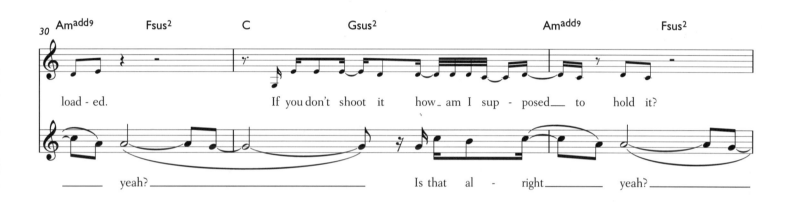

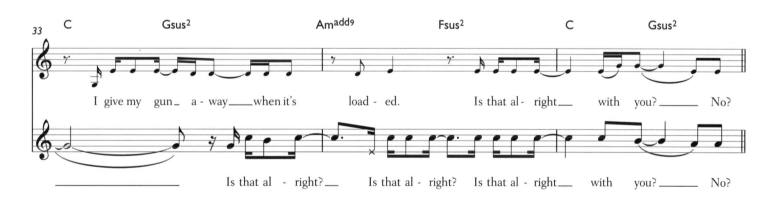

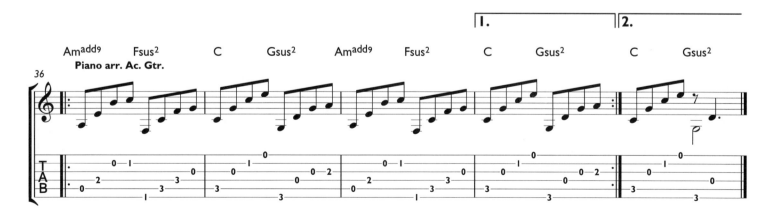

THE ANIMALS WERE GONE

Words and Music by Damien Rice

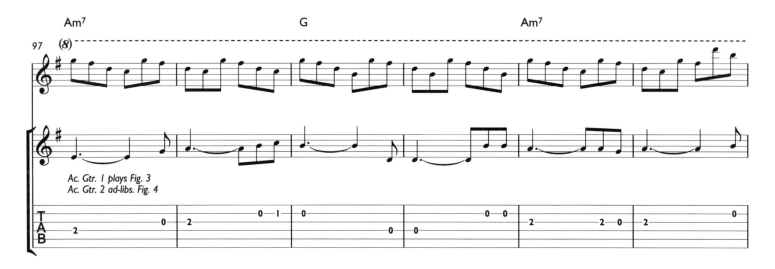

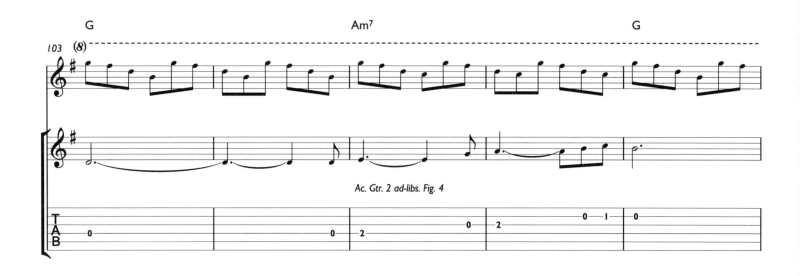

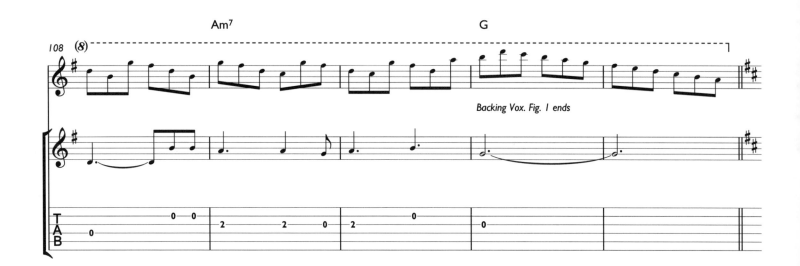

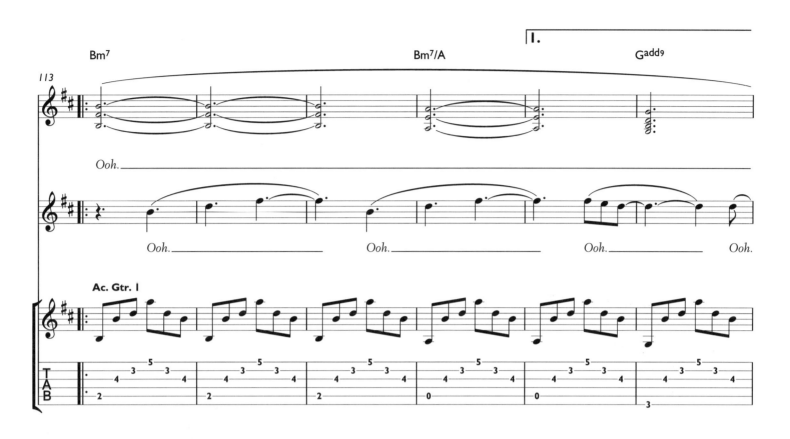

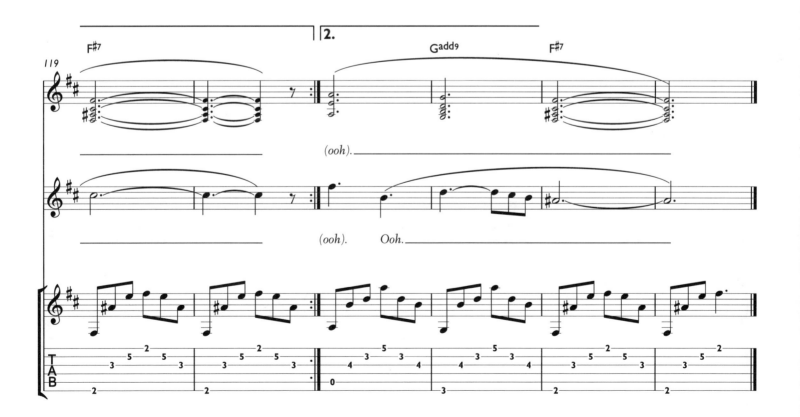

ELEPHANT

Words and Music by Damien Rice

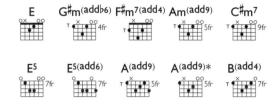

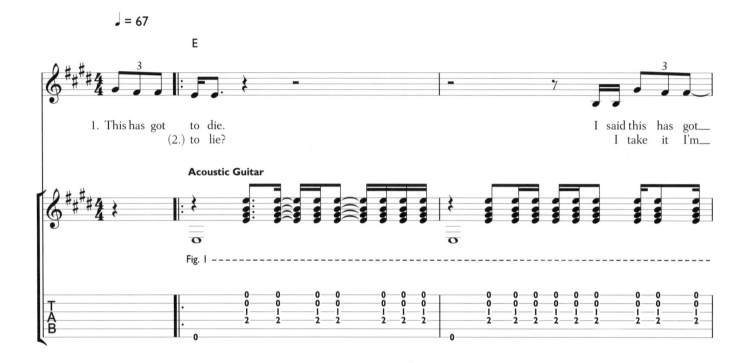

1. This has got to die.
(2.) to lie?

I said this has got___
I take it I'm___

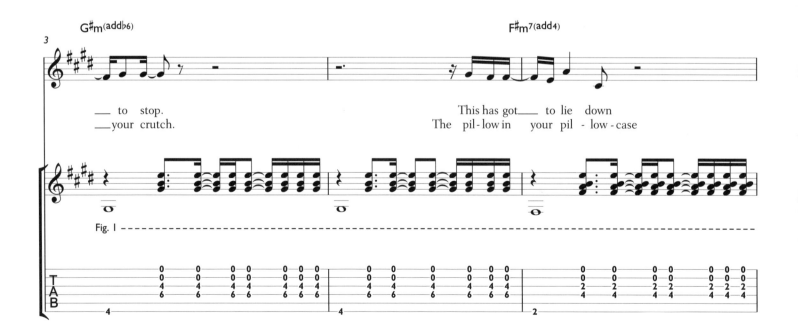

___ to stop.
___your crutch.

This has got___ to lie down
The pil-low in your pil-low-case

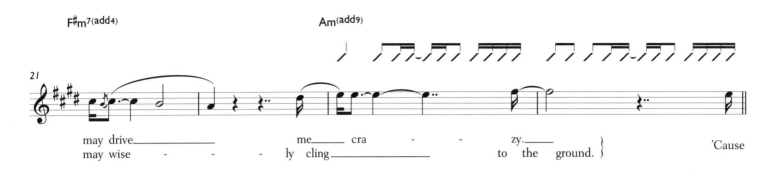

may drive_____ me____ cra - zy.____
may wise - - ly cling_____ to the ground. } 'Cause

I_____ am____ late - ly

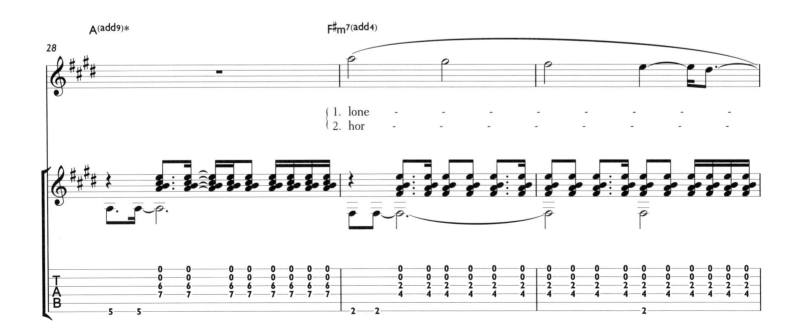

{ 1. lone - - - - - -
{ 2. hor - - - - - -

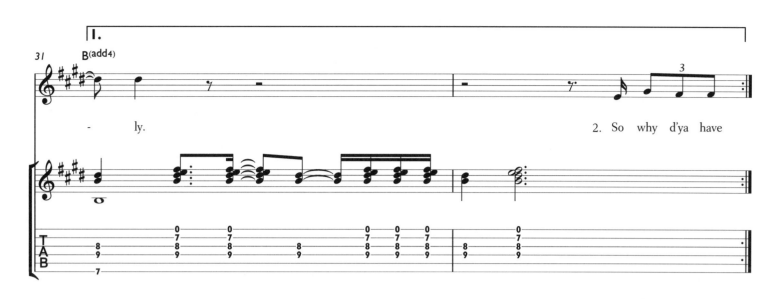

1.

ly.

2. So why d'ya have

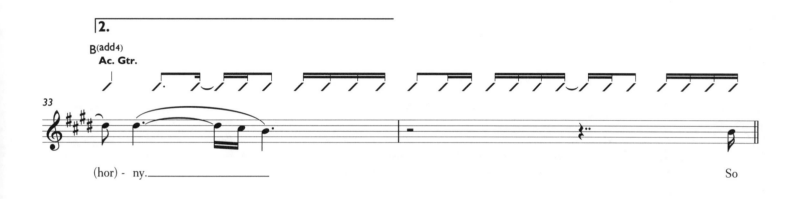

2.

B(add4)
Ac. Gtr.

(hor) - ny.

So

E5   E5(add6)   A(add9)   A(add9)*

why   would she take me

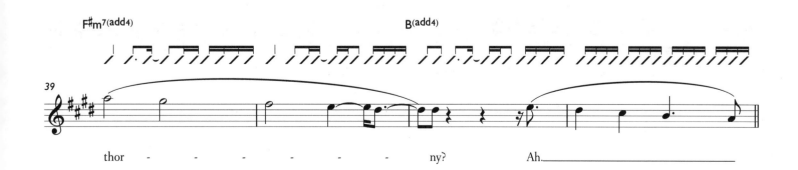

F#m7(add4)   B(add4)

thor - - - - - ny?   Ah.

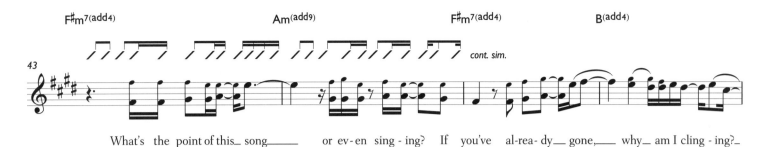

What's the point of this song___ or ev-en sing-ing? If you've al-rea-dy___ gone,___ why___ am I cling-ing?

___ Well I could___ throw her out,___ and I could___ live with-out and I could do it all___ for you.

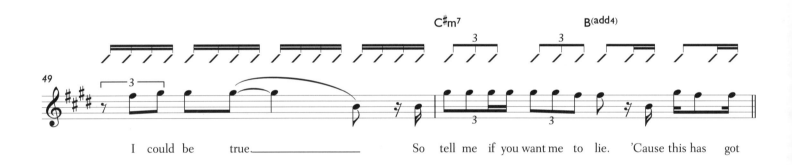

I could be true._____ So tell me if you want me to lie. 'Cause this has got

to die._____ I said this has got to stop.

Ac. Gtr.

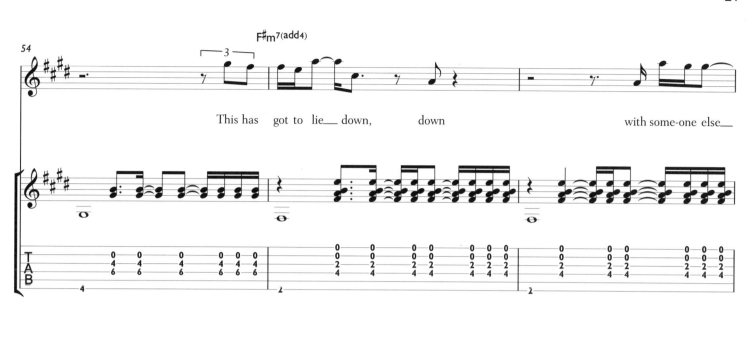

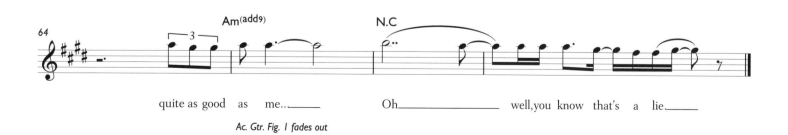

ROOTLESS TREE

Words and Music by Damien Rice

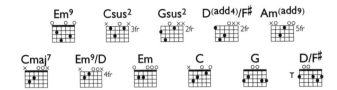

Capo guitar fourth fret

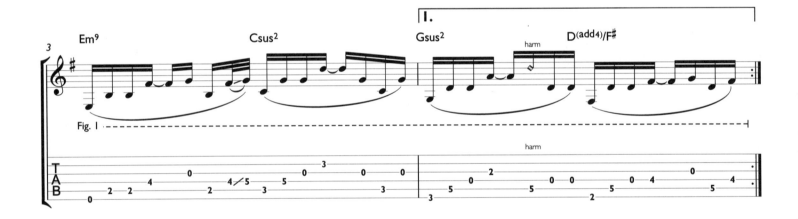

1. What I want ___ from you ___ is

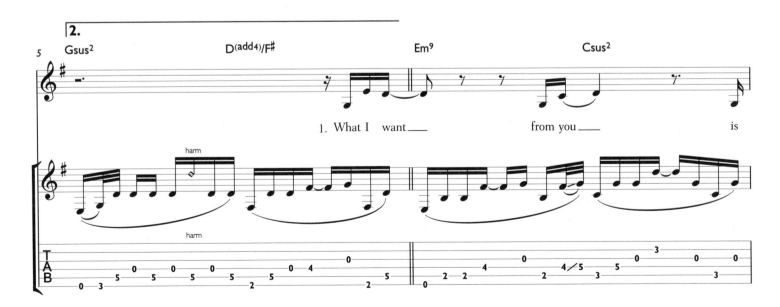

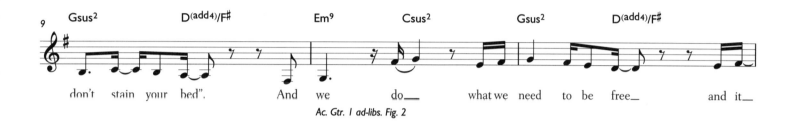

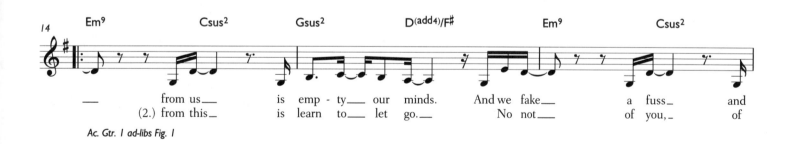

DOGS

Words and Music by Damien Rice

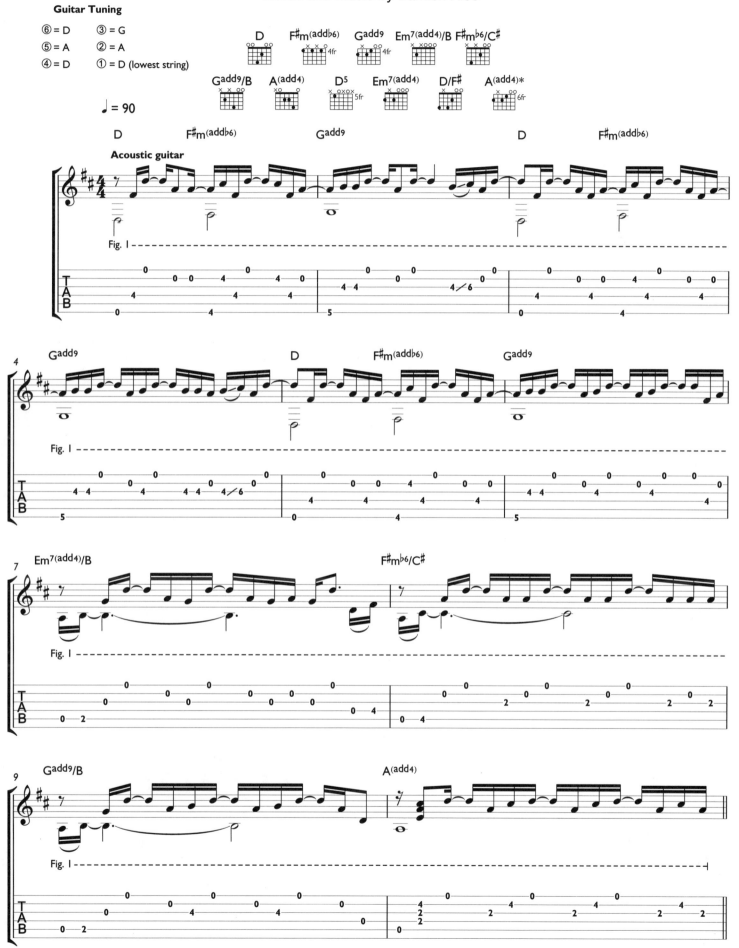

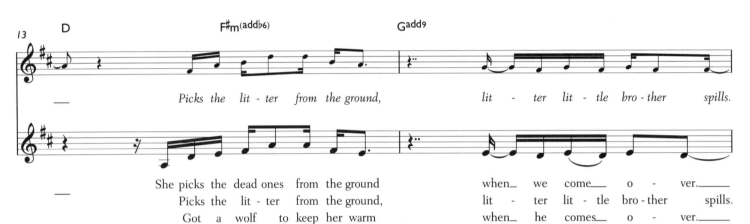

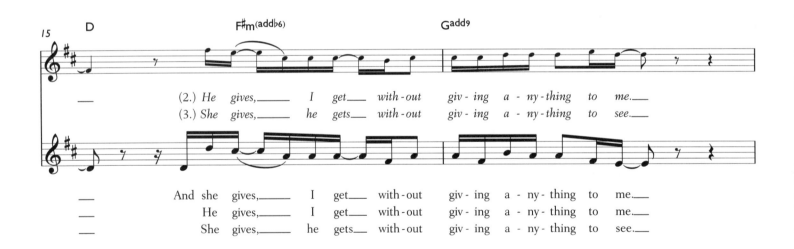

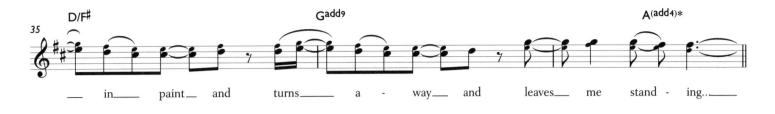

in paint and turns a - way and leaves me stand - ing...

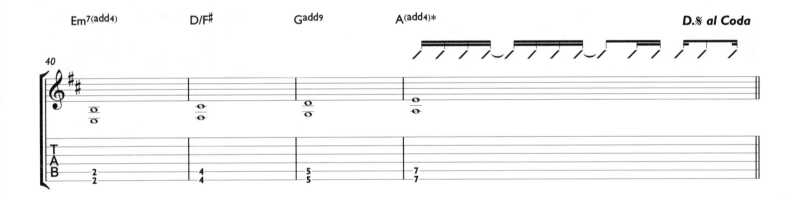

(yoga.)

COCONUT SKINS

Words and Music by Damien Rice

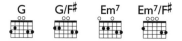

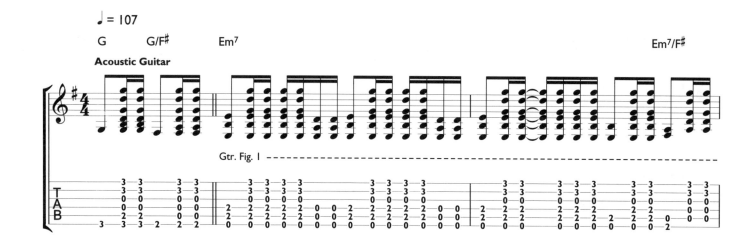

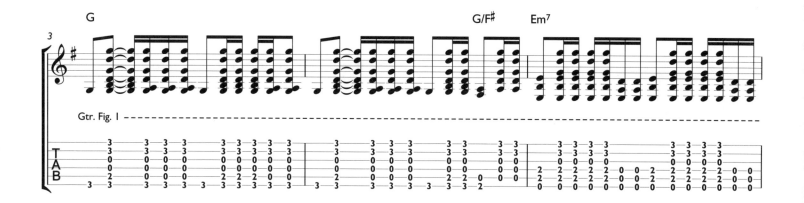

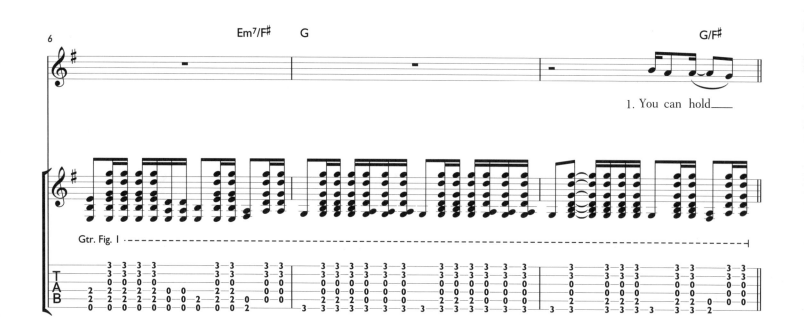

1. You can hold____

ME, MY YOKE & I

Words and Music by Damien Rice

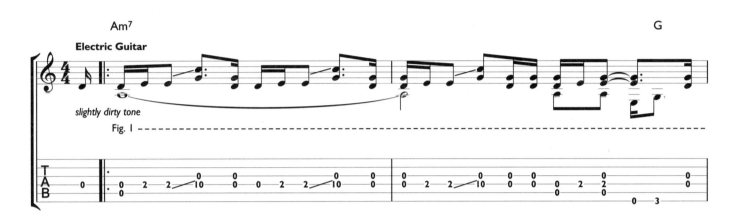

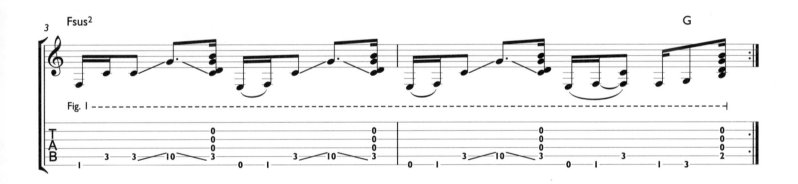

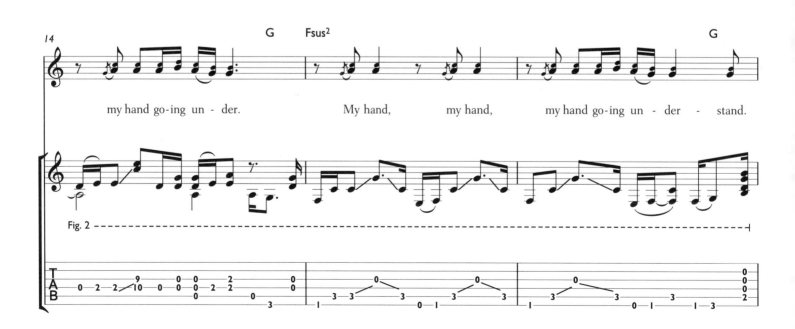

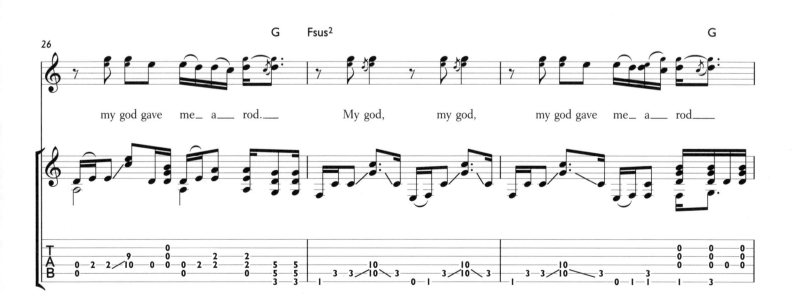

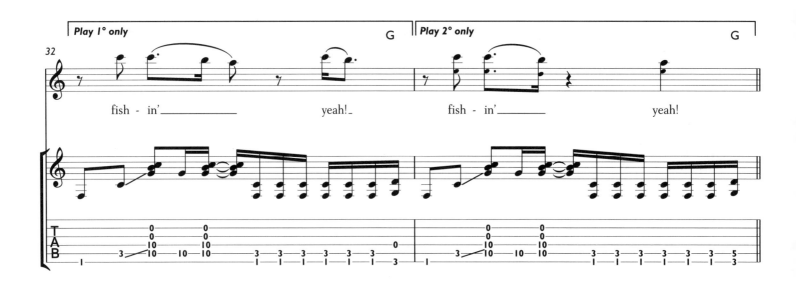

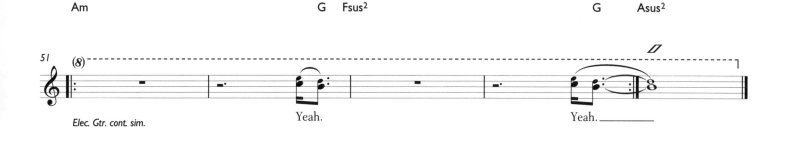

GREY ROOM

Words and Music by Damien Rice

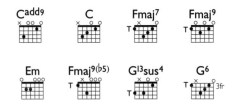

Where I___ stay in all day___ | I don't eat but I play__ with
Where I___ stay up all night___ | and all__ that I__ write__ is a

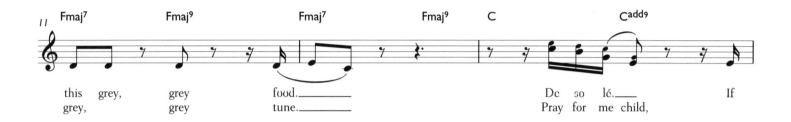

this grey, grey | food.___ | De so lé.___ | If
grey, grey | tune.___ | Pray for me child,

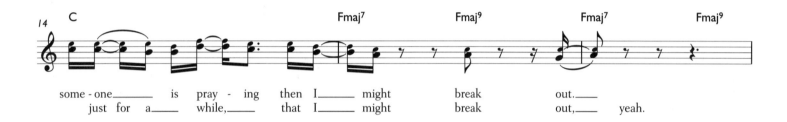

some - one___ is pray - ing then I__ might break out.___
just for a__ while,___ that I__ might break out,___ yeah.

De - so - lé.___ | Ev - en if I scream, I can't__ scream that loud. }
Pray for me child, | ev - en___ a smile__ would do for now. }

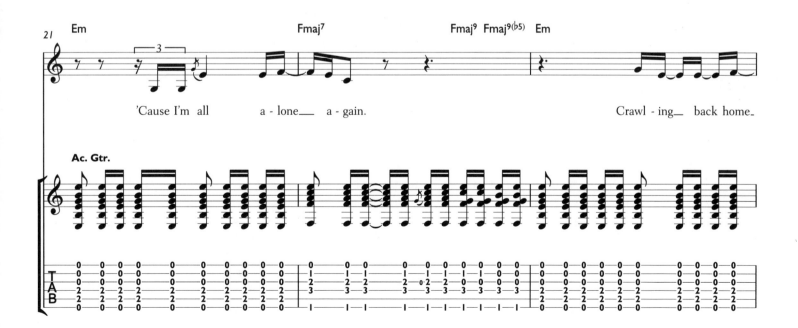

'Cause I'm all a - lone__ a - gain. | Crawl - ing__ back home_

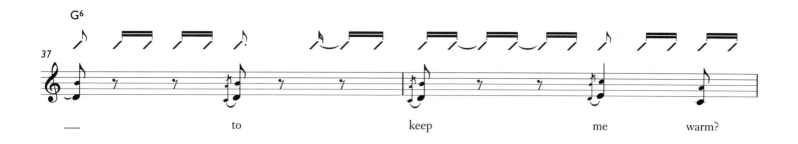

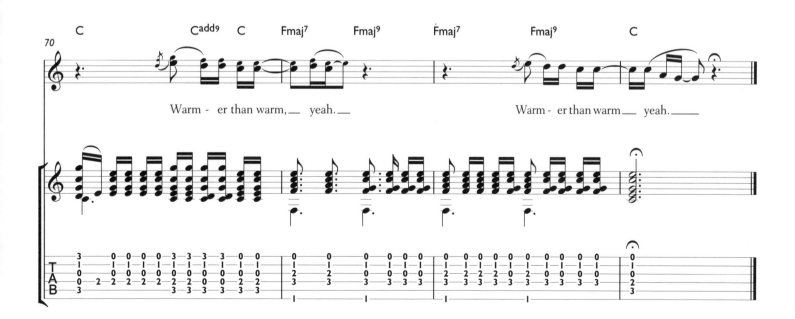

ACCIDENTAL BABIES

Words and Music by Damien Rice

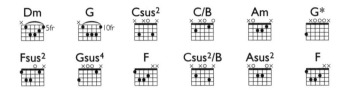

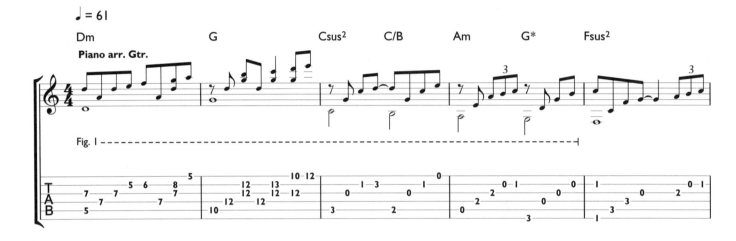

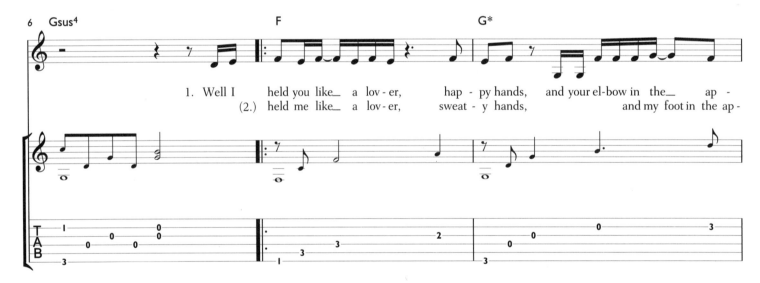

1. Well I held you like a lov-er, hap-py hands, and your el-bow in the ap-
(2.) held me like a lov-er, sweat-y hands, and my foot in the ap-

- pro-pri-ate place.   And we ig-nored our o-thers' hap-py
- pro-pri-ate place.   And we used cush-ions to cov-er hap-py

48

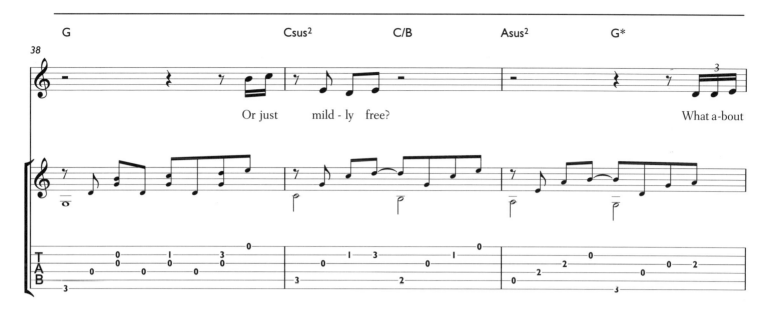

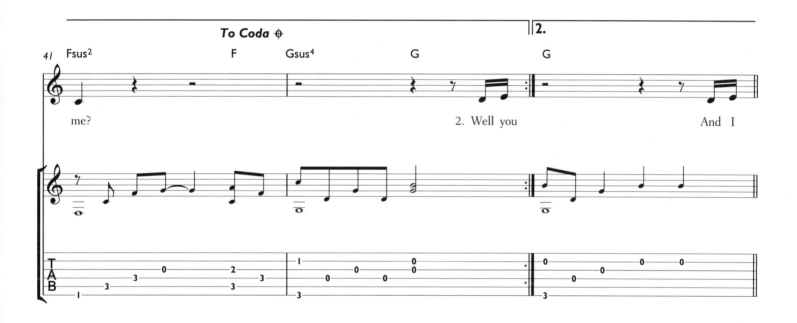

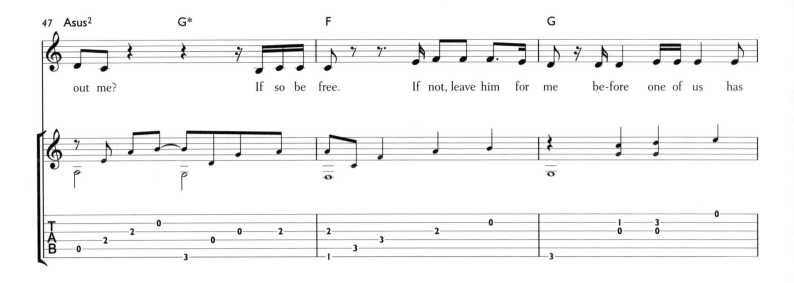

out me?   If so be free.   If not, leave him   for me   be-fore   one of us   has

D.%. al Coda

ac-ci-den   -   tal ba-bies.   For we are..._____   Do you

⊕ Coda

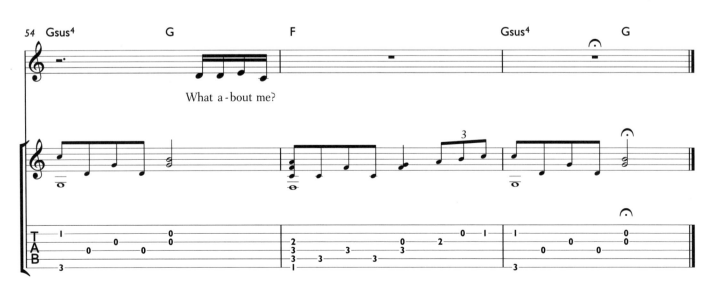

What a-bout me?

SLEEP, DON'T WEEP

Words and Music by Damien Rice

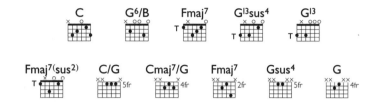

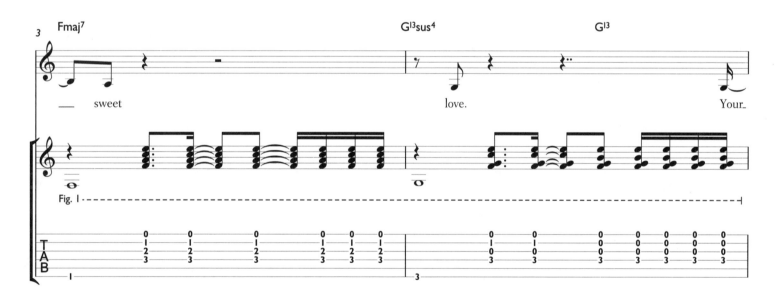

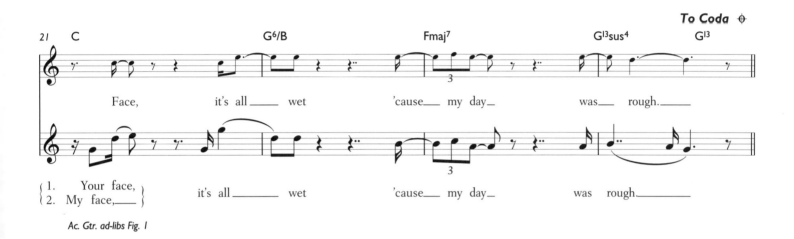

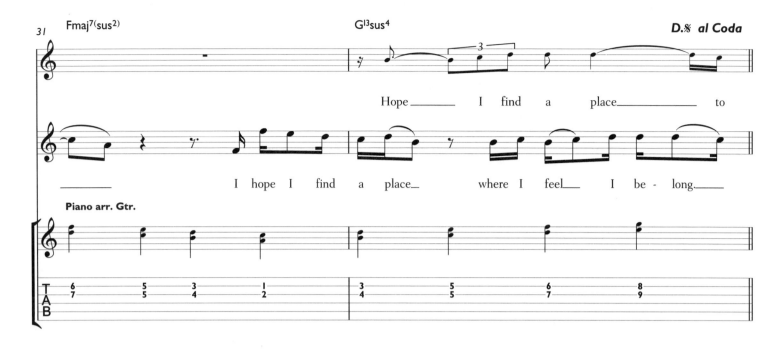

♦ Coda

Ac. Gtr. ad-libs. Fig. 1
2° & 3° Piano arr. Gtr. plays Fig. 4

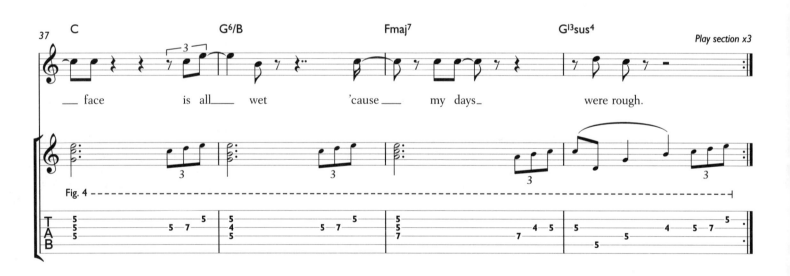

girl cutting grapefruit
for breakfast
she caught me watching
and her family turned
& looked

embarrassed I turned quickly
and stared into space

Notation and Tablature explained

Understanding chord boxes

Chord boxes show the neck of your guitar as if viewed head on—the vertical lines represent the strings (low E to high E, from left to right), and the horizontal lines represent the frets.

An **X** above a string means 'don't play this string'.
An **O** above a string means 'play this open string'.
The black dots show you where to put your fingers.

A curved line joining two dots on the fretboard represents a 'barre'. This means that you flatten one of your fingers (usually the first) so that you hold down all the strings between the two dots at the fret marked.

A fret marking at the side of the chord box shows you where chords that are played higher up the neck are located.

Tuning your guitar

The best way to tune your guitar is to use an electronic tuner. Alternatively, you can use relative tuning; this will ensure that your guitar is in tune with itself, but won't guarantee that you will be in tune with the original track (or any other musicians).

How to use relative tuning

Fret the low E string at the 5th fret and pluck; compare this with the sound of the open A string. The two notes should be in tune. If not, adjust the tuning of the A string until the two notes match.

Repeat this process for the other strings according to this diagram:

Note that the B string should match the note at the 4th fret of the G string, whereas all the other strings match the note at the 5th fret of the string below.

As a final check, ensure that the bottom E string and top E string are in tune with each other.

Detuning and Capo use

If the song uses an unconventional tuning, it will say so clearly at the top of the music, e.g. '6 = D' (tune string 6 to D) or 'detune guitar down by a semitone'. If a capo is used, it will tell you the fret number to which it must be attached. The standard notation will always be in the key at which the song sounds, but the guitar tab will take tuning changes into account. Just detune/add the capo and follow the fret numbers. The chord symbols will show the sounding chord above and the chord you actually play below in brackets.

Use of figures

In order to make the layout of scores clearer, figures that occur several times in a song will be numbered, e.g. 'Fig. 1', 'Fig. 2', etc. A dotted line underneath shows the extent of the 'figure'. When a phrase is to be played, it will be marked clearly in the score, along with the instrument that should play it.

Reading Guitar Tab

Guitar tablature illustrates the six strings of the guitar graphically, showing you where you put your fingers for each note or chord. It is always shown with a stave in standard musical notation above it. The guitar tablature stave has six lines, each of them representing a different string. The top line is the high E string, the second line being the B string, and so on. Instead of using note heads, guitar tab uses numbers which show the fret number to be stopped by the left hand. The rhythm is indicated underneath the tab stave. Ex. 1 (below) shows four examples of single notes.

Ex. 2 shows four different chords. The 3rd one (Asus4) should be played as a barre chord at the 5th fret. The 4th chord (C9) is a half, or jazz chord shape. You have to mute the string marked with an 'x' (the A string in this case) with a finger of your fretting hand in order to obtain the correct voicing.

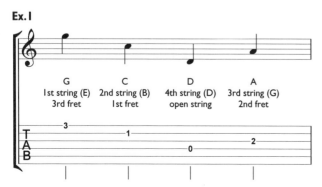

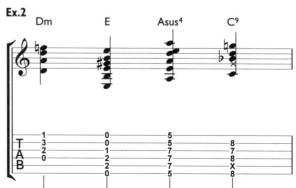

Notation of other guitar techniques

Picking hand techniques:

1. Down and up strokes
These symbols show that the first and third notes are to be played with a down stroke of the pick and the others up strokes.

2. Palm mute
Mute the notes with the palm of the picking hand by lightly touching the strings near the bridge.

3. Pick rake
Drag the pick across the indicated strings with a single sweep. The extra pressure will often mute the notes slightly and accentuate the final note.

4. Arpeggiated chords
Strum across the indicated strings in the direction of the arrow head of the wavy line.

5. Tremolo picking
Shown by the slashes on the stem of the note. Very fast alternate picking. Rapidly and continuously move the pick up and down on each note.

6. Pick scrape
Drag the edge of the pick up or down the lower strings to create a scraping sound.

7. Right hand tapping
'Tap' onto the note indicated by a '+' with a finger of the picking hand. It is nearly always followed by a pull-off to sound the note fretted below.

8. Tap slide
As with tapping, but the tapped note is slid randomly up the fretboard, then pulled off to the following note.

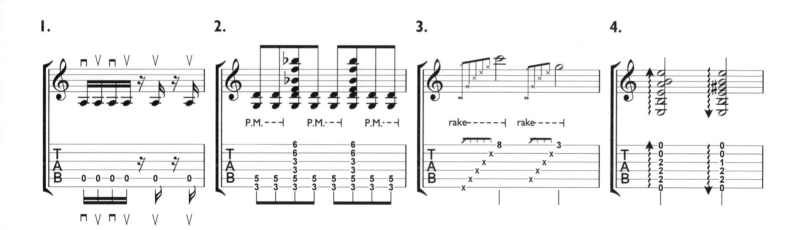

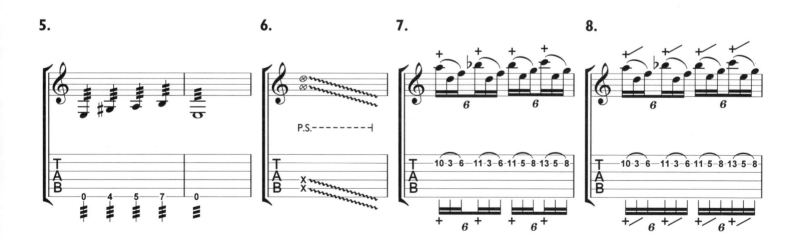

Fretting hand techniques:

1. Hammer-on and pull-off
These consist of two or more notes linked together by a slur. For hammer-ons, fret and play the lowest note, then 'hammer on' to the higher note with another finger. For a pull-off, play the highest note then 'pull off' to a lower note fretted with another finger. In both cases, only pick the first note.

2. Glissandi (slides)
Fret and pick the first note, then slide the finger up to the second note. If they are slurred together, do not re-pick the second note.

3. Slow glissando
Play the note(s) and slowly slide the finger(s) in the direction of the diagonal line(s).

4. Quick glissando
Play the note(s) and immediately slide the finger(s) in the direction of the diagonal line(s).

5. Trills
Play the note and rapidly alternate between this note and the nearest one above in the key signature. If a note in brackets is shown before, begin with this note.

6. Fret hand muting
Mute the notes with cross noteheads with the fretting hand.

7. Left hand tapping
Sound the note by tapping or hammering on to the note indicated by a 'o' with a finger of the fretting hand.

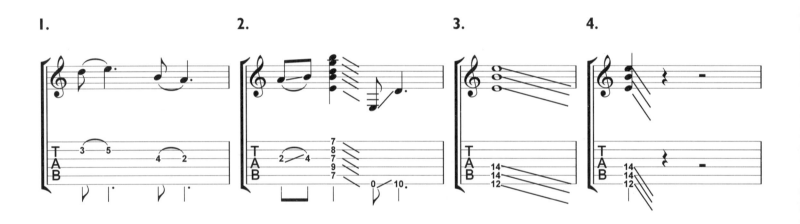

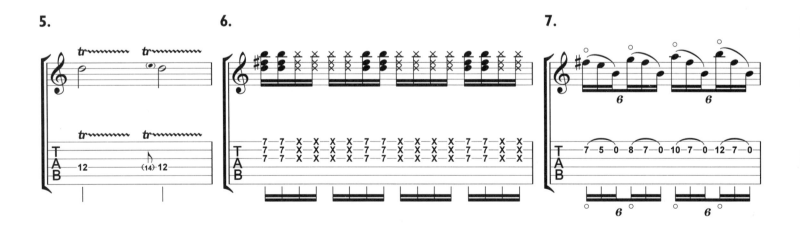

Bends and vibrato

Bends

Bends are shown by the curved arrow pointing to a number (in the tab).
Fret the first note and then bend the string up by the amount shown.

1. Semitone bend (half step bend)

The smallest conventional interval; equivalent to raising the note by one fret.

2. Whole tone bend (whole step bend)

Equivalent to two frets.

3. Minor third bend (whole step and a half)

Equivalent to three frets.

4. Microtonal bend (quarter-tone bend, Blues curl)

Bend by a slight degree, roughly equivalent to half a fret.

5. Bend and release

Fret and pick the first note. Bend up for the length of the note shown. May be followed by a release—letting the string fall back down to the original pitch.

6. Ghost bend (prebend)

Fret the bracketed note and bend quickly before picking the note.

7. Reverse bend

Fret the bracketed note and bend quickly before picking the note, immediately let fall back to the original.

8. Multiple bends

A series of bends and releases joined together. Only pick the first note.

9. Unison bend

Strike both indicated notes simultaneously and immediately bend the lower string up to the same pitch as the higher one.

10. Double note bend

Play both notes and bend simultaneously by the amount shown.

11. Bend involving more than one note

Bend first note and hold the bend whilst striking a note on another string.

12. Bends involving stationary notes

Play notes and bend lower string. Hold until release is indicated.

13. Vibrato

Shown by a wavy line. The fretting hand creates a vibrato effect using small, rapid up and down bends.

14. Bend and tap technique

Play and bend notes as shown, then sound final pitch by tapping onto note as indicated.

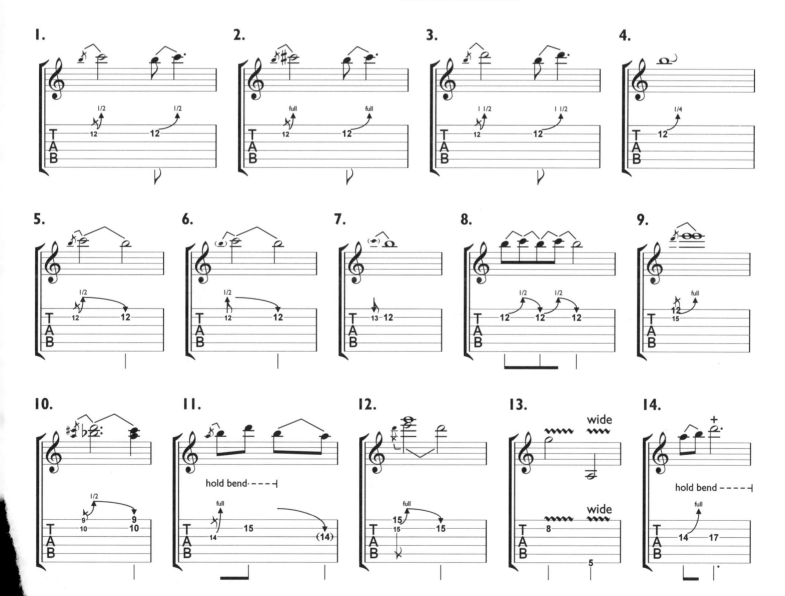

Tremolo arm (wammy bar)

1. Vibrato with tremolo arm
Create vibrato using small, rapid inflections of the tremolo arm.

2. Tremolo arm dive and return
Play note and depress tremolo arm by degree shown. Release arm to return to original note.

3. Tremolo arm scoop
Depress the arm just before picking the note and release.

4. Tremolo arm dip (or doop)
Pick the note, then lower the arm and quickly release.

5. Sustained note and dive bomb
Play note, hold for length of time shown and then depress arm to lower the pitch until the strings go slack.

6. Gargle
Pick the note and flick the tremolo arm rapidly with the same hand, making the pitch quiver.

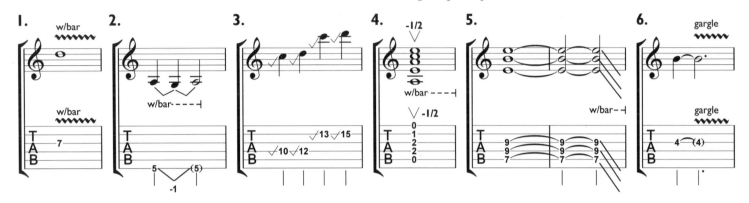

Harmonics & Other techniques

1. Natural harmonics
Instead of fretting properly, touch the string lightly with the fretting hand at the fret shown in the tab. Pick as normal. Diamond noteheads show the resultant pitch.

2. Artificial harmonics
The first tab number is fretted and held with the fretting hand as normal. The picking hand then produces a harmonic by using a finger to touch the string lightly at the fret shown by the bracketed number. Pick with another finger of the picking hand.

3. Pinched harmonics
Fret the note as shown, but create a harmonic by digging into the string with the side of the thumb as you pick it.

4. Tapped harmonics
Fret the note as shown, but create the harmonic through tapping lightly with the picking hand at the fret shown in brackets.

5. Touch harmonics
Fret the first note, hold it, then touch the string lightly at the fret shown at the end of the slur with the picking hand.

6. Violining
Turn the volume control to zero, pick the notes and then turn the control to fade the note in smoothly.

7. Fingering (fretting hand)
Small numbers show the finger with which each note is to be fretted.

8. Fingerpicking notation (PIMA)
Notation that shows which finger should be used to pick each note when playing finger style. p = thumb, i = index, m = middle, a = ring.

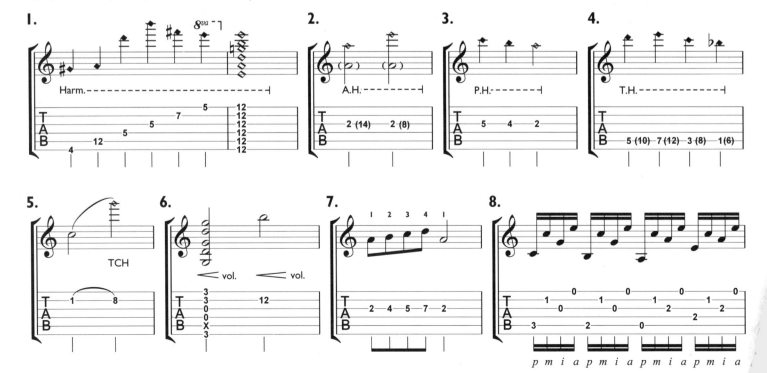